# PEGASUS ENCYCLOPEDIA LIBRARY

# Physics
# LIGHT AND COLOUR

Edited by: Anil Kumar Tomar, Pallabi B. Tomar
Managing editor: Tapasi De
Designed by: Vijesh Chahal, Anil Kumar and Rohit Kumar
Illustrated by: Suman S. Roy, Tanoy Choudhury
Colouring done by: Vinay Kumar, Sonu, Kiran Kumari & Pradeep Kumar

LIGHT AND COLOUR

# CONTENTS

What is light?......................................................................3

Blue skies and red sunsets.............................................. 4

Properties of light .............................................................5

Reflection of light............................................................. 8

Refraction ...........................................................................9

Dispersion of light by a prism ..................................... 12

Rainbow ........................................................................... 14

Mirages ............................................................................ 16

Mirrors ............................................................................. 17

Uses of the Mirrors ....................................................... 18

Image formation by concave mirrors.........................20

Image formation by convex mirrors...........................22

Lenses ..............................................................................24

Microscope .....................................................................26

Telescope ........................................................................28

Test Your Memory .........................................................31

Index .................................................................................32

# What is light?

Light is a kind of energy that radiates or travels in the form of waves. It is an electromagnetic wave that is, a wave of vibrating electric and magnetic fields. It is one of the small parts of the electromagnetic spectrum. Visible light is the part of the electromagnetic spectrum that our eyes can see. Light from the sun or a light bulb looks white, but it is actually a combination of many colours. By splitting the light with a prism, we can see the different colours of the spectrum. The rainbow in the sky is the natural example of this where colours of spectrum are visible.

The colours have different wavelengths, frequencies and energies. The energy of the radiation depends on its wavelength and frequency. Wavelength is defined as the distance between the crests of the waves and frequency is the number of waves that pass by each second. The wavelength and frequency of waves are inversely related. The longer is the wavelength of the light, the lower will be its frequency. And, also the less energy it will contain. Violet colour has the shortest wavelength in the visible spectrum. So, it has the highest frequency and energy. On the other end, red colour has the longest wavelength and lowest frequency and energy.

Light travels in space in a straight line if nothing disturbs it. For example, when light moves through the atmosphere, it continues to go straight until it bumps into a bit of dust or a gas molecule. The speed of light is 299,792 km/sec.

# LIGHT AND COLOUR

Light bends when it passes from one medium to another. This phenomenon is called **refraction**. When light enters a denser medium from less dense medium, it bends toward a line normal to the boundary between the two media. The greater is the density difference between the two media, the more the light will bend. This property is commonly used in optical devices such as microscopes, corrective lenses for vision, magnifying lenses and many more others.

Total internal reflection is the phenomenon that combines both refraction and reflection of light. When light coming from the air strikes water, a part is reflected and a part is refracted. When the angle of incidence of the light striking the water is more than the critical angle, it gets totally reflected and in fact, cannot leave the water. Fibre optics uses this property of light to keep light beams focused without significant loss, as long as the bending of the cable is not too sharp. For example, television and telephone cables use fibre optic cables more and more as they make transmission much faster and more efficient.

**Dispersion** of light refers to the ability to split white light into its constituent colours. White light consists of all of the colours we are able to see. When white light enters a prism, the spectrum of light emerges from the other side as a beam of multi-coloured light. Violet light, with longer wavelengths, gets bent more by the different angles of the prism than red light and the other colours are in between violet and red on the wave spectrum.

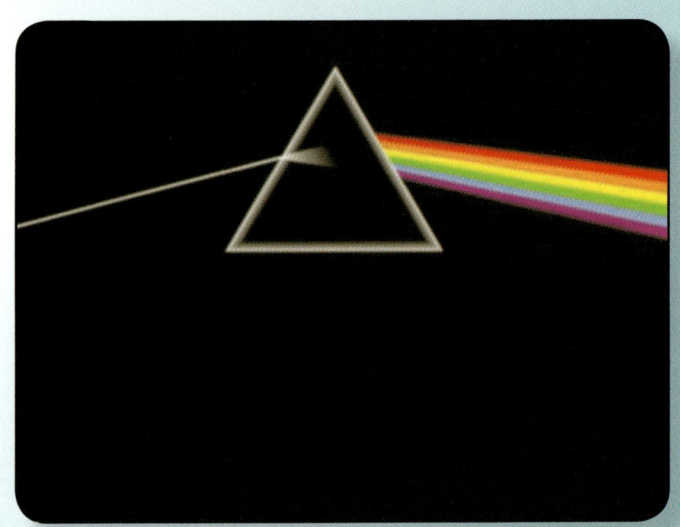

## Do it yourself

**Water prism:** Set a tray of water in sunlight. Lean a mirror against an inside edge and adjust so that a rainbow appears on the wall. You can also use a light bulb shining through a slit in a flat cardboard piece as a light source.

# Properties of light

A rainbow is a natural phenomenon that exemplifies most of the properties of light. It uses refraction, dispersion and internal reflection to produce their amazing colour hues. When white light enters raindrops from the sun, it gets dispersed and refracted inside the raindrops. The dispersed light hits the back of the raindrop and gets internally reflected. Rainbows are considered one of the most beautiful examples of optics in nature.

**Diffraction** is another property of light which refers to the fact that light bends as it goes through an opening. When there is a light source shielded by a door such that only a limited amount of light can get through the opening, diffraction can occur. Sound waves can describe this in better way. If someone speaks standing in front of an open door, a person standing way around the corner from the door will still hear the diffracted sound waves.

**Interference of light** occurs when two beams of light meet in a system. Depending on the nature of the two beams and when they meet, they can either be constructive or destructive. If they merge and enhance one another and give a brighter beam, it is called constructive interference. If they interfere in such a way as to make the merged beam less bright, it is called destructive interference.

# Reflection of light

When light reflects from a smooth surface such as a mirror, the wave that strikes the surface is called the incident ray, and the one that bounces back is called the reflected ray. An imaginary line perpendicular to the point at which the incident wave strikes the reflecting surface is called the normal. The angle between the incident ray and the normal is called the angle of incidence and the angle between the reflected ray and the normal is called the angle of reflection. Reflected light obeys the law of reflection which states that the angle of reflection equals the angle of incidence. The angle of incidence and reflection of a light are represented as $\Theta_i$ and $\Theta_r$ respectively. Thus, for smooth surfaces

$\Theta_i = \Theta_r$

The best surfaces for reflecting light are always very smooth, such as a glass mirror or polished metal. All the light travelling in one direction and reflecting from the mirror is reflected in one direction. Objects can be seen by the light they emit or by the light they reflect. The amount of incident-wave energy that is reflected from a surface depends on the nature of the surface and the angle at which the wave strikes the surface. The amount of wave energy reflected increases as the angle of incidence increases.

## 3D pictures and movies

3D films trick our brain, bringing images projected onto a flat cinema screen to life in full three dimensional glories. If we look at an object near us and close our left and right eyes in turn, we will see that each has a slightly different view of the world. Our left eye sees a bit more of the left side of the object and right eye sees a bit more of its right side. The brain fuses those two images together allowing us to see in three dimensions. This is well known as stereoscopic vision. To produce the similar effects, 3D films are captured using two lenses placed side by side, just like our eyes. This can also be done by producing computer generated images to replicate the same effect.

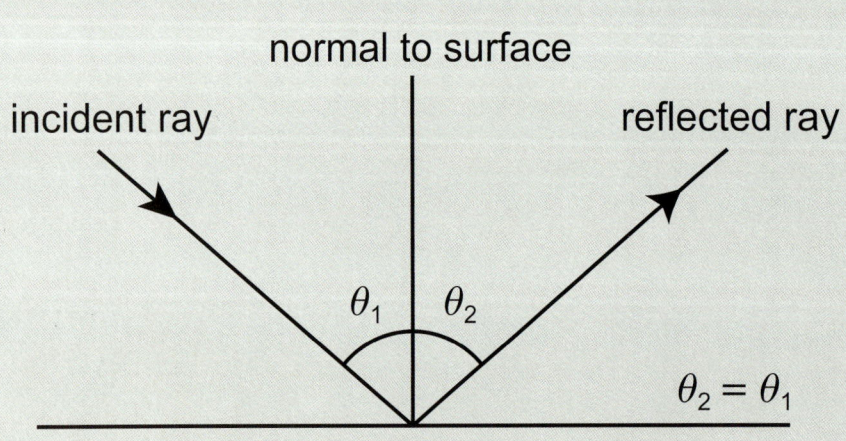

# Refraction

As light passes from one medium to another, its speed changes, and it bends. This is called refraction of light. It can be defined as the bending of a wave (light wave in our case) when it enters a medium where its speed is different. As the speed of light reduces in the slower medium, its wavelength also shortens proportionately. The frequency remains unchanged as it is a characteristic of the source of the light and independent to the medium. Refraction is responsible for image formation by lenses and the eye.

The bending depends on the refractive index of the mediums and the angle between the light ray and the line perpendicular to the surface separating the two mediums. Each medium has a different refractive index. The angle between the light ray and the normal as it leaves a medium is called the angle of incidence. The angle between the light ray and the normal as it enters a medium is called the angle of refraction.

For example, light entering or exiting a water surface is bent by refraction. The refractive index of water is 4/3, implying that light travels 3/4 as fast in water as it does in vacuum. When we submerge a pencil in a glass of water, it appears as broken inside water. This happens due to refraction of light at the water surface.

Submerged objects always appear to be shallower than they are because the light from them changes angle at the surface.

## Laws of refraction

There are two basic laws of refraction. Refraction of light waves is governed by these two laws.

1. The incident ray, refracted ray and the normal at the point of incidence lie in the same plane.

2. The ratio of sine of the angle of incidence with the sine of the angle of refraction for a given pair of media is always constant. This law is commonly known as the Snell's law.

$\sin \Theta_i / \sin \Theta_r = $ constant

# LIGHT AND COLOUR

Mathematically, we can quantify the degree of refraction using the following equation

$n = c/v$

Where,

c is the speed of light in a vacuum, $3 \times 10^8$ m/sec

v is the average speed of light in the optically dense medium

n is a dimensionless quantity known as medium's refraction index

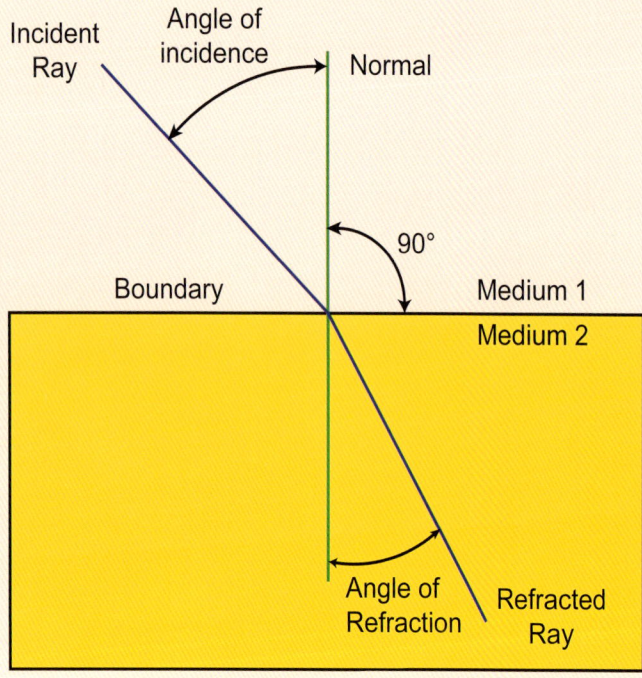

## Total internal reflection

Total internal reflection is defined as complete reflection of a ray of light within a medium such as water or glass from the surrounding surfaces back into the medium. Total internal reflection is an optical phenomenon that occurs when a ray of light strikes a medium boundary at an angle larger than the critical angle with respect to the normal to the surface. For a water-air surface the critical angle is 48.5°. As the indices of refraction depend on wavelength, the critical angle (and hence the angle of total internal reflection) will vary slightly with wavelength. At all angles less than the critical angle, both refraction and reflection occur in varying proportions.

When light crosses a boundary between materials with different refractive indices,

### Do it yourself

**Mixing colours:** Find three flashlights. Cover each with coloured cellophane or paint the plastic lenscover with nail polish (red, green and blue). Shine onto a white ceiling or wall, overlap the colours and make new colours. Leave the flashlights on, line them up on a table, turn off the lights, and dance - you will be making rainbow shadows onthe wall! In addition, you can paint the lens of a fourth flashlight yellow.

# Refraction

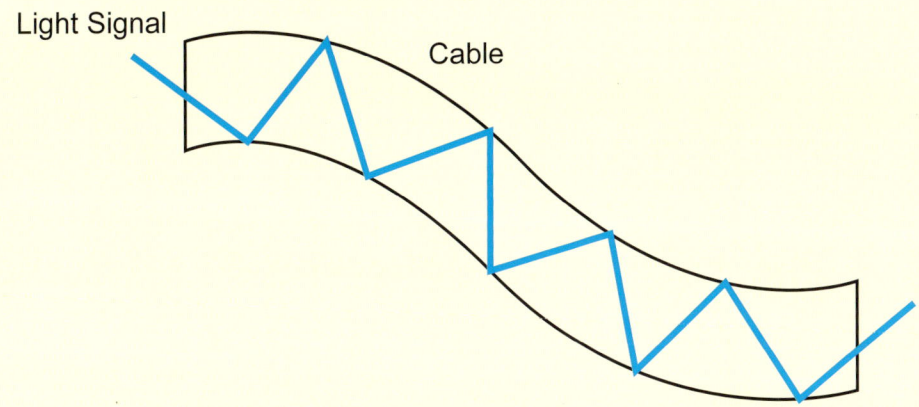

the light beam will be partially refracted at the boundary surface and partially reflected. However, if the angle of incidence is greater than the critical angle, the light will stop crossing the boundary altogether and instead totally reflect back internally. The critical angle is defined as the angle of incidence at which light is refracted such that it travels along the boundary. Total internal reflection can only occur when light travels from a medium with a higher refractive index to one with a lower refractive index. For example, it can only occur when passing from glass to air, but not when passing from air to glass.

The natural phenomena such as halos and rainbows are examples of total internal reflections in ice crystals and water droplets. Glass prisms can be shaped to produce total internal reflection and are employed in binoculars, periscopes, telescopes, and other optical instruments. Light rays may be conducted over long, twisting paths by multiple total internal reflections in glass or plastic rods or fibres.

## What causes a shadow?

In a darkened room, shine a strong flashlight or a shaded lamp bulb on a white wall, or on a sheet tacked to the wall, as in the illustration. Place the lamp 5 to 10 feet from the wall. Stand behind the lamp. Do you make a shadow? Hold up your hand, or stand between the lamp and the wall. What happens? Move farther away from the light and closer to the wall and see what happens to the shadow?

Result: You will see that you do not cast a shadow when you stand behind the light. You cast a big shadow when you stand near the light and far from the wall. As you move farther from the light, the shadow becomes smaller.

Explanation: You cast a shadow by blocking the rays of light. As you move away from the source of light, your shadow becomes smaller because you cut off fewer of the light rays. Any object that does not permit light to pass through creates a shadow.

LIGHT AND COLOUR

# Rainbow

One of nature's most splendid masterpieces is the rainbow. A rainbow is an excellent demonstration of the dispersion of light and one more piece of evidence that visible light is composed of a spectrum of wavelengths, each associated with a distinct colour. Each individual droplet of water acts as a tiny prism that disperses the light and reflects it back to our eyes. The net effect of the vast array of droplets is that a circular arc of VIBGYOR is seen across the sky.

A rainbow occurs when raindrops and sunlight cross paths. When sunlight enters water drops and passes through the droplets, the light separates into its component colours. This is similar to the effect of a glass prism. A rainbow is usually seen in the opposite direction in the sky from the sun. The rainbow light

is reflected to the eye at an angle of 42 degrees to the original ray of sunlight. As the 42 degree angle is measured from each individual observer's eye, no two people see exactly the same rainbow. If you travel towards the end of a rainbow, it will move ahead of you, maintaining its shape.

The bright, primary rainbow has red on the outer edge and blue within. Higher in the sky there is always another, dimmer rainbow with the order of colours reversed. This secondary rainbow results from additional reflection of sunlight through the raindrops. Rainbows are not limited to the dispersion of light by raindrops. The splashing of water at the base of a waterfall caused a mist of water in the air that often results in the formation of rainbows. Bright sunlight, suspended droplets of water and the proper angle of sighting are the three necessary components for viewing a rainbow.

## Rainbow formation

1. On a rainy day, there are plenty of raindrops in the atmosphere. The sunlight should strike a raindrop at a certain angle before a rainbow is possible.

2. Some of the light gets reflected and rest of the light gets refracted.

3. White light splits into its constituent colours by dispersion.

4. At the rear of the raindrop, the light hits the water-air interface. If the angle of incidence is greater than the critical angle, total internal reflection occurs. A rainbow can only be seen if this happens; otherwise the light will continue out the other side of the raindrop and continue to move away.

5. As the speed of light changed when it entered the raindrop, its speed changed again when it leaves the raindrop. Thus, light is refracted again as it left the raindrop. Here, the light moves from a denser medium (water) to a less denser medium (air). So, it speeds up and its path bends.

6. As the rays are refracted once again, colours are further dispersed. This increases the separation of the component colours of white light and a beautiful rainbow of clearly separated

# LIGHT AND COLOUR

# Mirages

A mirage is phenomenon of optical illusion. For example, illusionary water spots seen in deserts and on the roads in summers. That 'wet' looking spot in the deserts or on the road up ahead could actually be a mirage that stays in the distance, as impossible to reach as a rainbow. So, a mirage is an optical phenomenon that creates the illusion of water. It results from the refraction of light through a non-uniform medium.

Mirages are most commonly observed on sunny days when driving down a roadway. As we drive down the roadway, there appears to be a pool of water on the road several hundred metres ahead in front of the car. When we reach out to that point, it moves ahead and we never reach the spot of that water pool. This appearance of the water pool is simply an illusion. On a sunny day, sun heats the roadway to high temperatures which in turn heats the surrounding air. We know that, hot air is less optically dense than cooler air. As a result, a non-uniform medium has been created by the heating of the roadway and the air just above it. So, light travelling in a straight line through a uniform medium, refracts when reaches through a non-uniform medium. When the refracted ray meets our eyes, it appears to be coming from the road surface instead of the distant sky and a 'mirage' is seen.

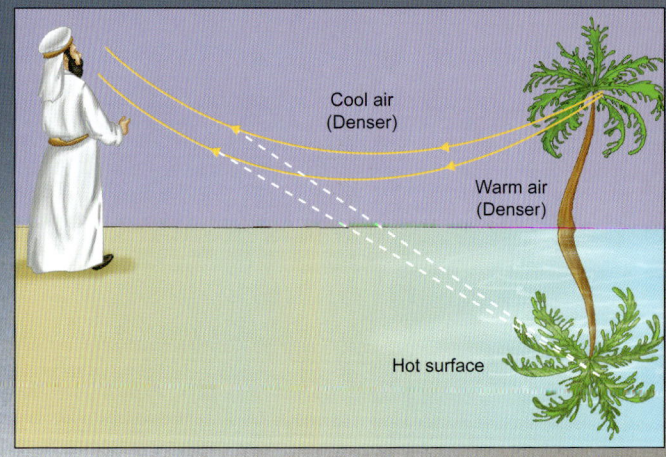

# Mirrors

A mirror is highly polished surface that can help a person view the exact shape, size and features of the body. When light rays fall on the polished surfaces, the rays reflect due to the reflective surface provided by mirrors. There are three types of mirrors— plain, concave and convex.

All the mirrors are used for different purposes as they all are different in shape and rays falling on them bounce back in different ways. The plain mirror has a flat surface. The concave mirrors are curved inwards, while the convex mirrors are bulged outside.

A light ray that falls on plane mirror, bounces off without suffering a bend or a curve. As a result, the mirror image retains similar features of the shape as the original. As the concave mirrors are bent inwards, the light rays diverge from the curve of this mirror. The image formed by the concave mirror is inverted when the object is far away. In other cases, it appears erect and magnified. Light rays diverge when they are reflected from the curved surface of the convex mirror. As a result of this, the rays converge to a point and help the viewer see the image. The images formed by the convex mirror are erect and they appear farther than they actually are.

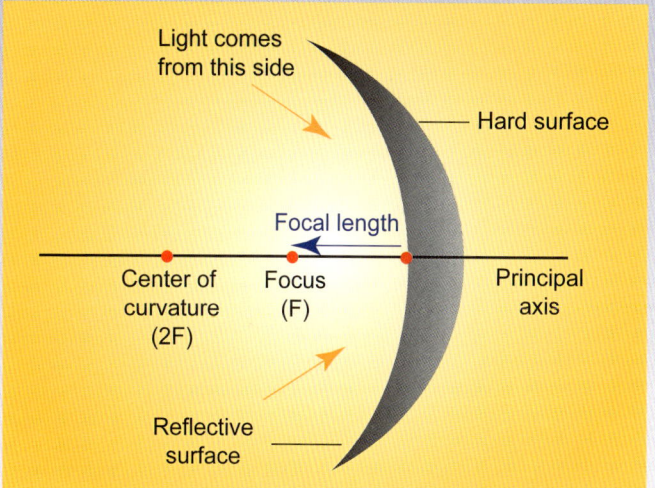

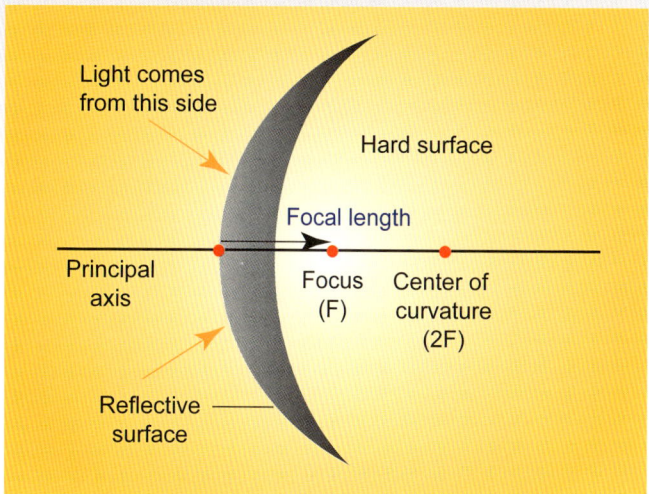

# Uses of mirrors

## Plane mirrors

- They are used as looking glasses as dressing table mirrors, washbasin mirrors and mirrors in saloons
- They are used for making instruments like periscopes and kaleidoscopes
- They are also used to create illusions and effects

## Concave mirror

- They are used for converging of solar radiations in solar cookers to generate adequate heat for cooking purposes
- They are used by doctors to focus light on and magnify the images of internal body parts such as teeth, ear, nose and throat
- They are used as reflectors in projectors, lighthouse headlights, searchlights, torches, etc
- Large concave mirrors are used in reflecting telescopes

## Convex mirror

- Rear-view mirrors of cars use convex mirrors to produce an erect and diminished image of the objects approaching from behind
- They are used in streetlights to diverge light over an extended area

## Image formation by plane mirrors

In most cases, the mirrors are pieces of glass with a silvered coating on the back. Some objects may also behave like mirrors such as smooth surfaces of lakes and ponds, windows, sides of aquariums, etc. The following rays are usually considered while constructing ray diagrams of image formation by plane mirrors.

### Do it yourself

**Pinhole Camera:** Use a cardboard box that is light-proof (no leaks of light anywhere). Cut off one side of the box. Tape a piece of tracing paper over the cut-out side, keeping it taut and smooth. Make a pinhole in the side opposite the tracing paper. Point the pinhole at a window and move toward or away from the window until you see its image in clear focus on the tracing paper. You can hold up a magnifying glass in front of the pinhole to sharpen an image.

## Uses of mirrors

1. A ray of light that incidents on a plane mirror at 90 degree gets reflected along the same path.

2. A ray of light falling on a plane mirror follows the law of reflection. So a ray that incidents at any angle, gets reflected from the mirror such that the angle of incidence is equal to the angle of reflection. The image is formed at a point where the reflected rays appear to meet.

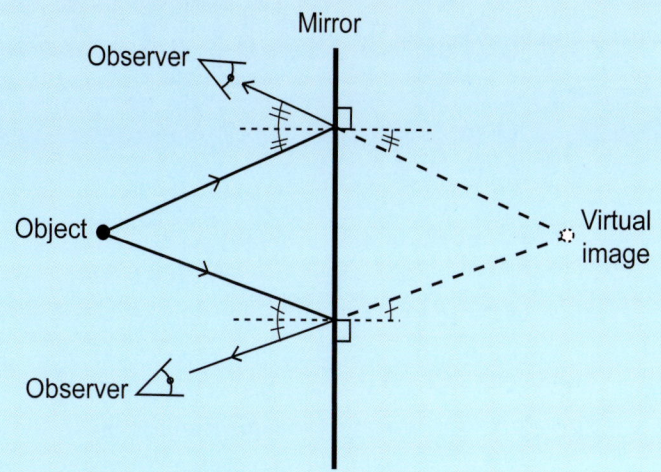

It has been established through a series of experiments with plane mirrors that if the mirrors are inclined at an angle $\Theta$ then the number of images is given by the relation

Number of images formed = $360/\Theta - 1$

If $360/\Theta$ is not a whole number, then the number of images will be equal to the nearest integer.

# Image formation by concave mirrors

## Case 1: When an object is placed at infinity

Let us consider two rays, one striking the mirror at its pole and the other passing through the centre of curvature. The ray which is incident at the pole gets reflected according to the law of reflection. It reflects back with an angle similar to the

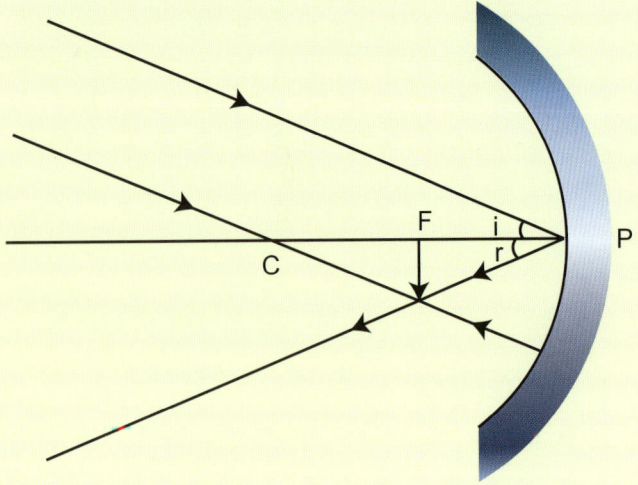

angle of incidence. The second ray which passes through the centre of curvature of the mirror retraces its path. These rays after reflection form an image at the focus. The image formed is real, inverted and diminished.

## Case 2: When the object is placed beyond the centre of curvature

We should consider two rays to obtain the image— the ray passing through the centre of curvature and the ray parallel to the principal axis. The ray passing through the centre of curvature retraces its path while the ray which is parallel to the principal axis passes through the focus after reflection. These rays after reflection form an image at a point between the centre of curvature and focus. The image is inverted, real and diminished.

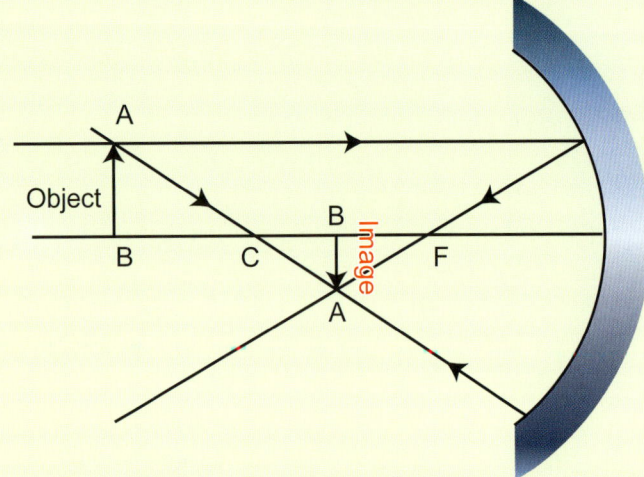

## Case 3: When the object is placed at the centre of curvature

Let us consider the two rays, one coming parallel to the principal axis and the other passing through the focus. The first ray passes through the focus after reflection. The other ray passing through the focus

# Image formation by concave mirrors

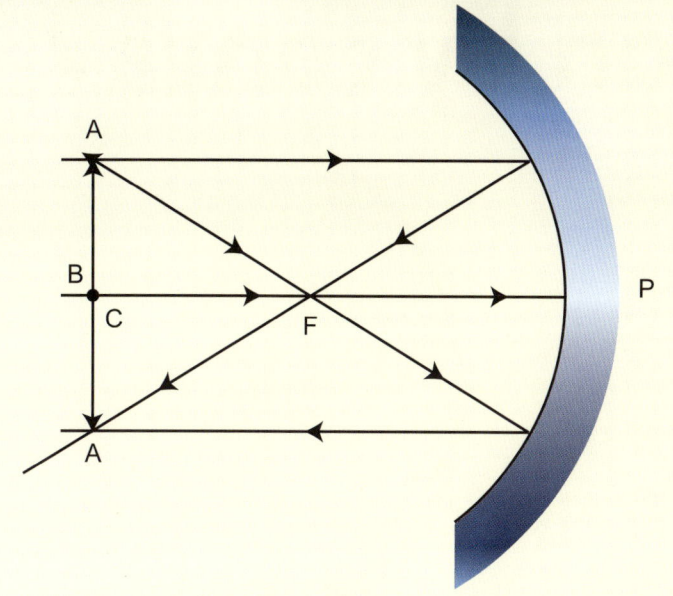

reflected rays are parallel to each other, thus, the image is formed at infinity. It is a real, inverted and enlarged.

## Case 5: When the object is between the pole and the focus

In this case, one ray of light is passing parallel to the principal axis and another ray is passing through the centre of curvature. The ray which is passing through the centre of curvature retraces its path while the other ray reflects through the focus. These rays appear to meet behind the mirror. Thus, the image formed is virtual, erect and magnified.

reflects parallel to the axis. These rays form an image at the centre of curvature. The image is inverted, real and of the same size as the object.

## Case 4: When the object is at the focus

In this case, one ray of light passes parallel to the principal axis reflects through the focus. Another ray passing through the centre of curvature retraces its path. The

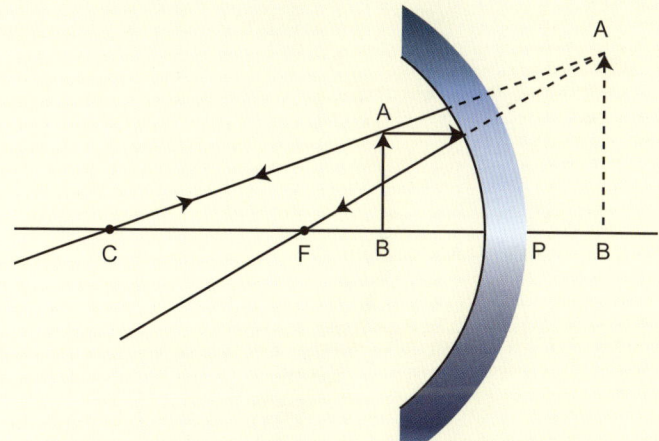

## Equation for the image formed by the concave mirror

$1/v + 1/u = 1/f$

v, u, and f are image distance, object distance, and focal length of the mirror respectively.

The magnification of image formed can be calculated as,

$m = -v/u$

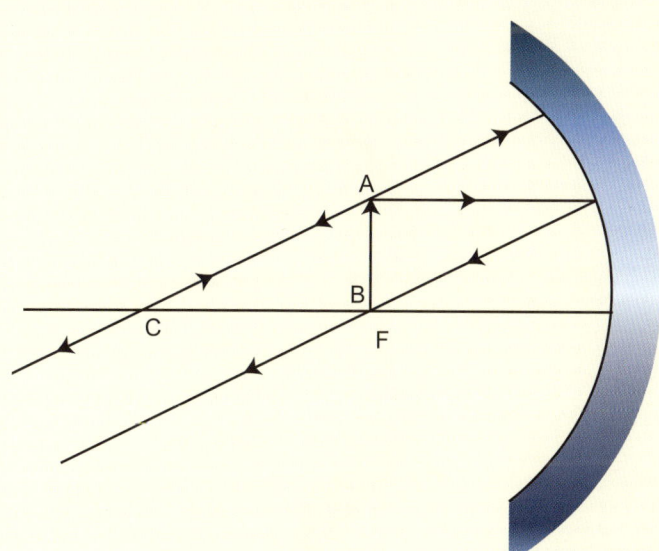

21

# Image formation by convex mirrors

A convex mirror is sometimes referred to as a diverging mirror due to the fact that incident light originating from the same point and will reflect off the mirror surface and diverge. The incident rays reflect through the convex mirrors in the following manner:

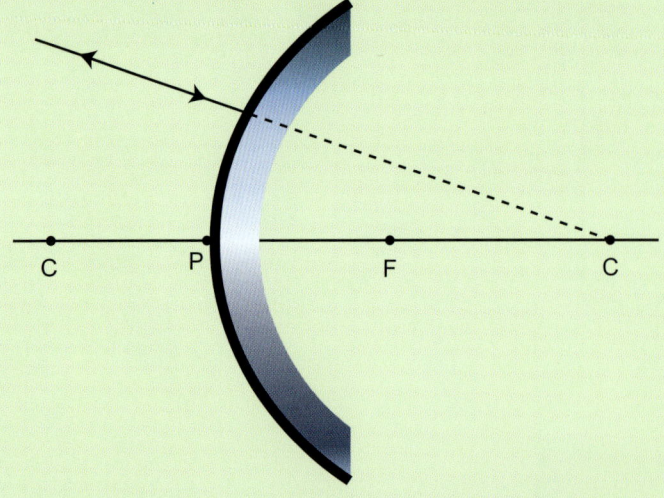

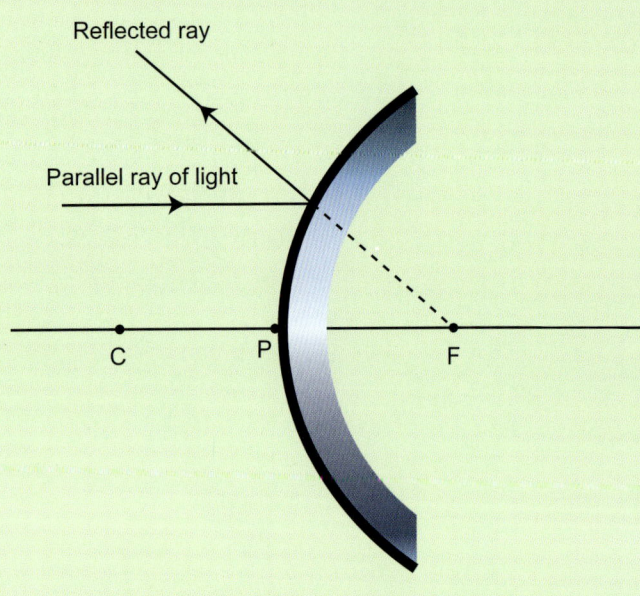

Following the previous facts, the images formed by convex mirrors can be described as:

**Case 1:** If the object is placed between pole and focus, the image also forms between the pole and the focus. The image formed is

- Erect
- Diminished
- Virtual

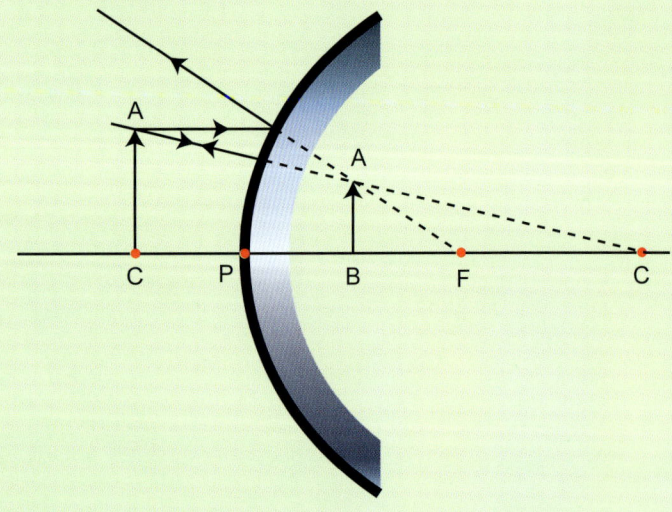

1. A ray of light travelling parallel to the principal axis, after reflection from a convex mirror it appears coming from its focus behind the mirror.

2. A ray of light travelling towards the centre of curvature behind the mirror hits the mirror at 90 degrees and reflects along its path.

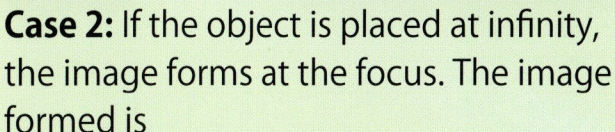

# Image formation by convex mirrors

**Case 2:** If the object is placed at infinity, the image forms at the focus. The image formed is

- Erect
- Diminished
- Virtual

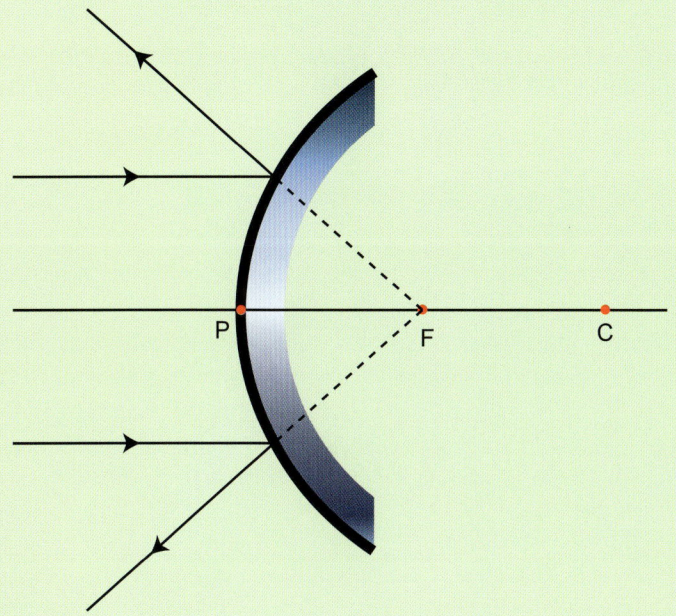

## Make a rainbow

Take a glass of water (about three quarters full) and white paper to a part of the room with sunlight (near a window is good). Hold the glass of water above the paper and watch as sunlight passes through the glass of water. It refracts and forms a rainbow of colours on sheet of paper. Try holding the glass of water at different heights and angles to see if it has a different effect.

Explanation: While you normally see a rainbow as an arc of colours in the sky, they can also form in other situations. You may have seen a rainbow in a water fountain or in the midst of a waterfall. Rainbows form in the sky when sunlight refracts as it passes through raindrops. It acts in the same way when it passes through glass of water. The sunlight refracts, separating it into the colours red, orange, yellow, green, blue, indigo and violet.

# Do it yourself

**Kaleidoscopes:** For these light experiments, carefully tape together three identical mirrors, making a triangle-tube with the mirrors on the inside. Tape all rough edges well and quickly look through the opening as you walk around.

# LIGHT AND COLOUR

# Lenses

Lenses are optical elements used to focus or defocus images. They are made up of high quality glass, plastics or polymers usually circular in shape and have two surfaces that are ground and polished in a specific manner designed to produce either a convergence or divergence of light. There are two basic types of lenses— concave lens and convex lens.

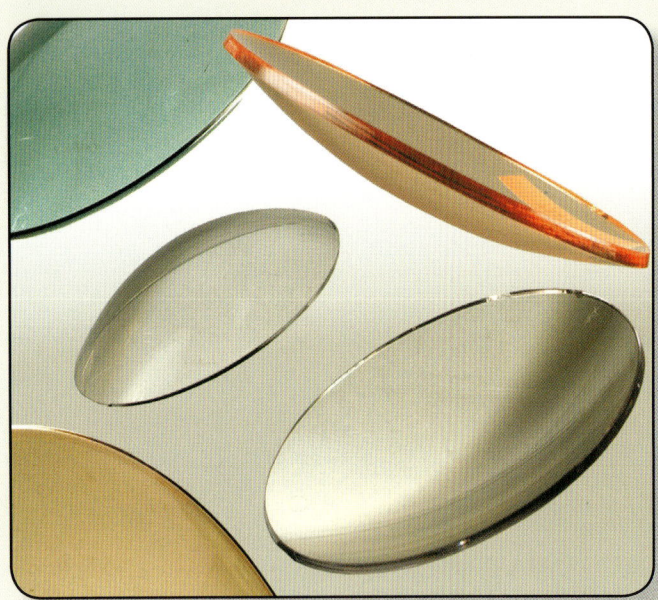

## Concave lenses

A concave lens is skinny in the middle and wide on the outside. Concave lenses are also known as negative lenses or diverging lenses. Concave lenses are generally prescribed for myopia or short-sightedness. The following rays are considered while constructing ray diagrams for images formed by a concave lens for the various position of the object.

1. An incident ray of light, coming parallel to the principal axis of a concave lens, appears to come from its focus after refraction.

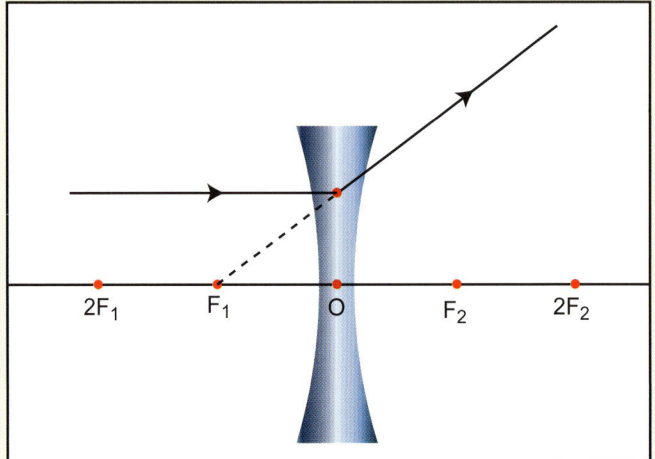

2. An incident ray of light passing through the optical centre refracts without any deviation.

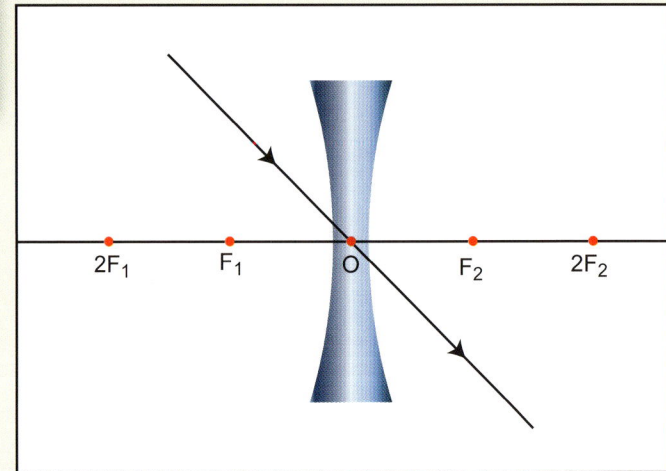

The images formed by a concave lens are always virtual, erect and diminished image whatever maybe the position of the object.

## Convex lens

A convex lens is thick at centre and thin at the edges. A convex lens is also called positive lens or converging lens, because it converges the rays of light falling on it. Convex lenses are generally prescribed for hypermytropia or long-sightedness.

A convex lens forms the image of an object if placed in front of it. Any point on the object acts as a point of source, from which an infinite number of rays start. The rays considered for constructing the ray diagrams of image formation by convex mirror follow the refraction as

1. A ray of light passing through the optical centre of the lens travels straight without suffering any deviation. This holds good only in the case of a thin lens.

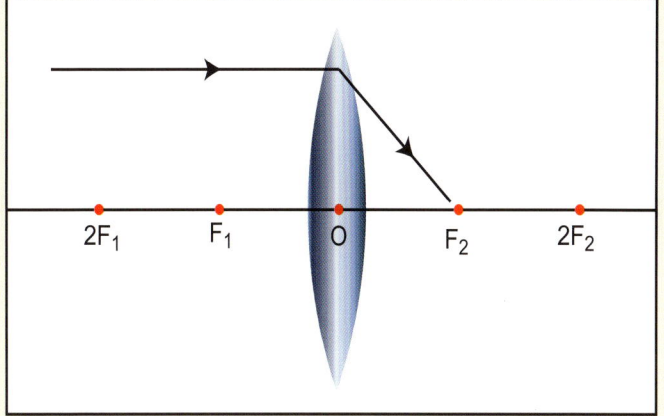

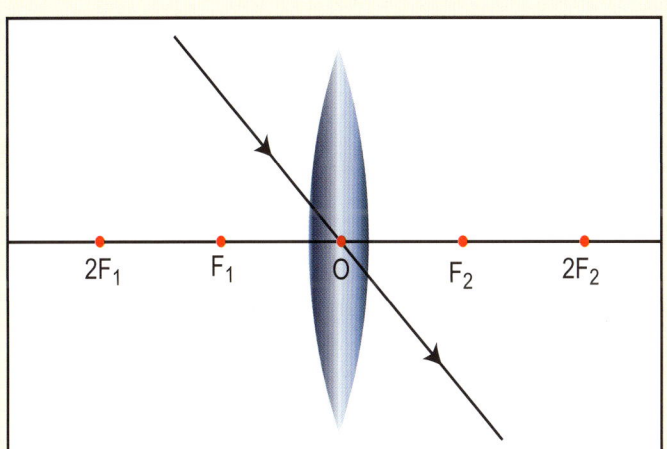

2. An incident ray parallel to the principal axis after refraction passes through the focus.

3. An incident ray passing through the focus of a lens emerges parallel to the principal axis after refraction.

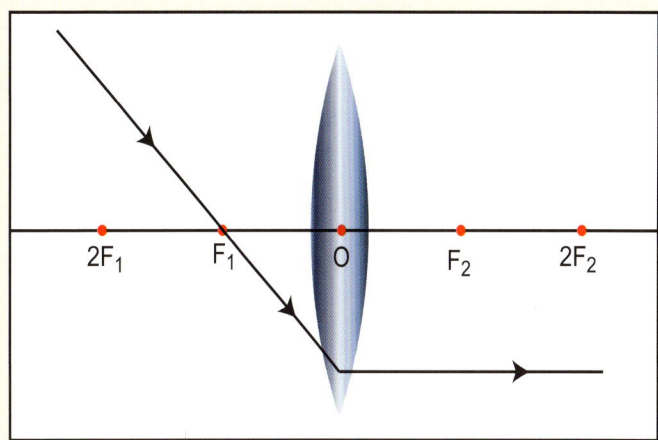

These basic assumptions are followed to construct the ray diagrams of the images formed by convex lenses. The nature of these images depends upon the distance of the object from the optical centre of the lens.

On a clear day, a beam of sunlight can be reflected off a mirror and seen up to 25 miles away.

LIGHT AND COLOUR

# Microscope

A compound microscope is an instrument that uses combination of two or more lenses to produce magnified images of small objects. Zaccharias Hanssen invented the first microscope in 1590. He used several lenses in a tube and found that the object at the end of the tube was magnified significantly beyond the capability of a magnifying glass. This was the beginning of microscopy and he proposed that an image magnified by a single lens can be further magnified by a second lens. Anthony Van Leeuwenhoek took the microscopy to the higher levels and invented many microscopes with highly improved resolving power. The simplest optical microscope is the magnifying glass and is good to about ten

### Do it yourself

**Microscope:** Hold one magnifying glass in each hand. Focus one lens on a printed letter or small object. Add the second lens above the first, so you can see through both. Move the lens toward and away from you until you bring the letter into clear focus again. You just made a microscope! The lens closest to your eye is the eyepiece. The lensclosest to the object is the objective.

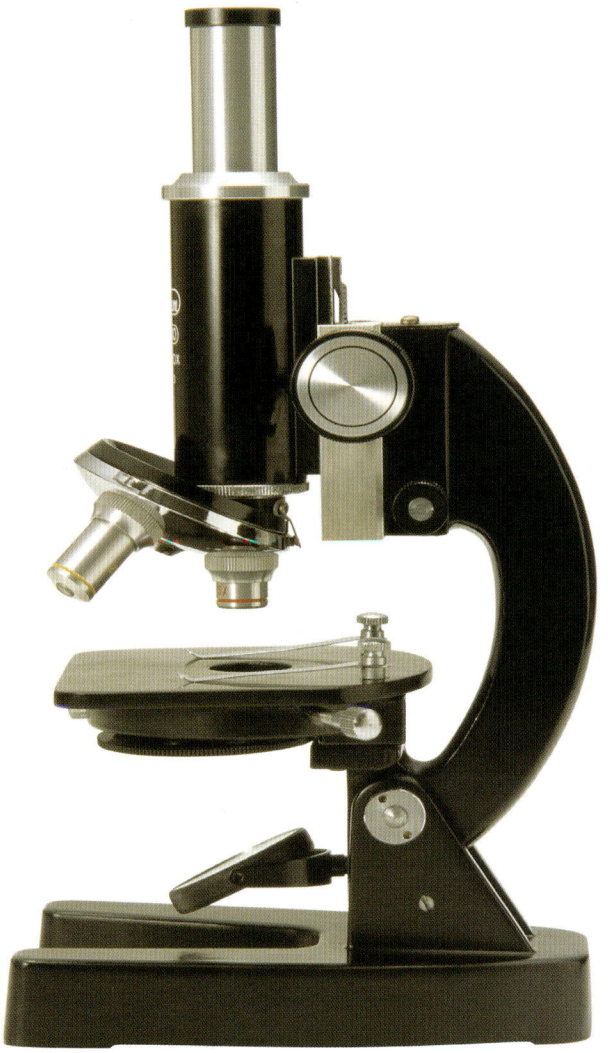

times (10X) magnification. The compound microscope has two systems of lenses for greater magnification:

1. The eyepiece lens
2. The objective lens

## Components of a microscope

We look through the **eyepiece** at the top of the microscope. A standard eyepiece has a magnifying power of 10x. Eyepiece tube holds the eyepieces in place above the objective lens.

**Objective lenses** are the primary optical lenses of a microscope. They range from 4x-100x and have three or four lens on most microscopes. Objectives can be forward or rear-facing.

**Nosepiece** houses the objective lenses. The objectives are exposed and are mounted on a rotating turret so that different objective lenses can be conveniently selected.

**Coarse and knobs** are used to focus the microscope. Nowadays, coaxial focus knobs are more convenient since the users do not have to grope for a different knob.

**Stage** is the part where the specimen is placed to view. **Stage Clips** are used to keep specimen slide undisturbed.

The hole in the stage through which the transmitted light reaches the stage is called **Aperture**.

**Illuminator** is the light source of a microscope located at the base of the microscope. Most light microscopes use low voltage bulbs with continuous variable lighting control.

**Condenser** collects and focuses the light from the illuminator on to the specimen.

**Iris Diaphragm** is located above the condenser and below the stage and controls the amount of light reaching the specimen.

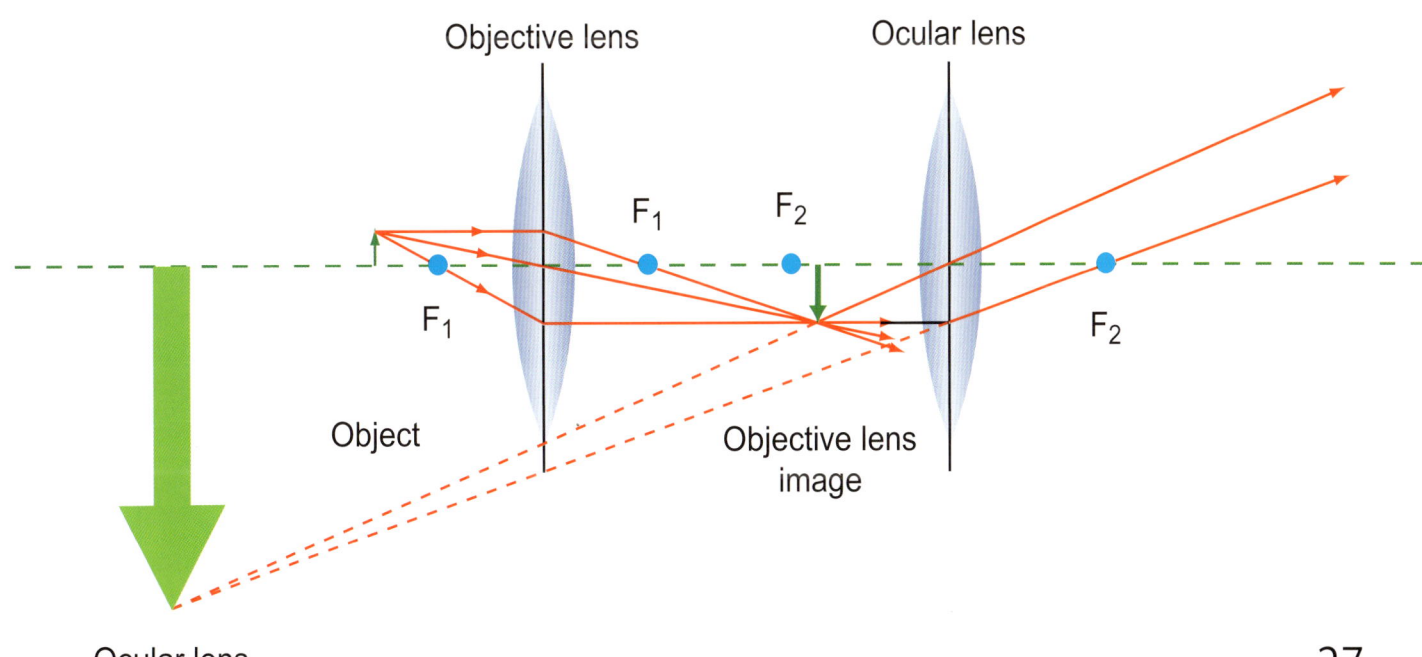

LIGHT AND COLOUR

# Telescope

Telescope is defined as an optical instrument which is used for observing distant objects. This is made up by combination of mirror or lenses which gather the visible light and make an object visualize bigger and nearer for easy observation. In 1608, the first telescope was invented by a Dutch lens grinder, Hans Lippershey. Two other inventors, Zacharias Janssen and Jacob Metius, are also credited for developing telescopes around the same time. Further improvements were made by Galileo Galilei who developed his own refractor telescope for astronomical studies in 1609. The British scientist Sir Isaac Newton constructed the first reflecting telescope using a concave primary mirror and a flat diagonal secondary mirror in the year 1668.

Telescopes generally consist of two lenses, one for capturing the distant image and another for viewing it as large image. There are two basic types of telescopes, refracting and reflecting. The part of the telescope that gathers the light, called the objective, determines the type of telescope. A refracting telescope uses a glass lens as its objective while a reflecting telescope uses a mirror as its objective.

## Do it yourself

**Dust helps us to see:** Arrange your window shades so that only a small ray of bright sunshine comes into the room. Follow the beam of light with your eye. You will see that you can see dust moving in the path of the ray of light.

**Explanation:** Dust particles reflect light and help us to see indoors and in other places where the sun does not shine directly.

## Travelling microscope

A common travelling microscope consists of a metal base fitted with three levelling screws. A matallic carriage, clamped to a spring loaded bar slides with its attached vernier and reading lens along an inlaid strip of metal scale. The scale is divided in half millimeters. Fine adjustments are made by means of a micrometer screw for taking accurate reading. Microscope tube consists of an Eyepice (generally 10x) and an Objective (15mm-75mm). The Microscope, with its rack and pinion attachment is mounted on a vertical slide, runs with an attached vernier along the vertical scale. The microscope is free to rotate in vertical plane. The vertical guide bar is coupled to the horizontal carriage of the microscope. For holding objects, a horizontal stage made up of a conolite sheet is always attached to the base.

## Inverted microscope

An inverted microscope is upside down compared to other conventional microscopes. The light source and condenser are on the top, above the stage and pointing down. The objectives are below the stage and pointing up. The specimens are placed on top of the stage as in the conventional microscopes. The binocular tube is in the standard position pointing at a conventional viewing angle. As a result, one is looking up through the bottom of whatever is holding the

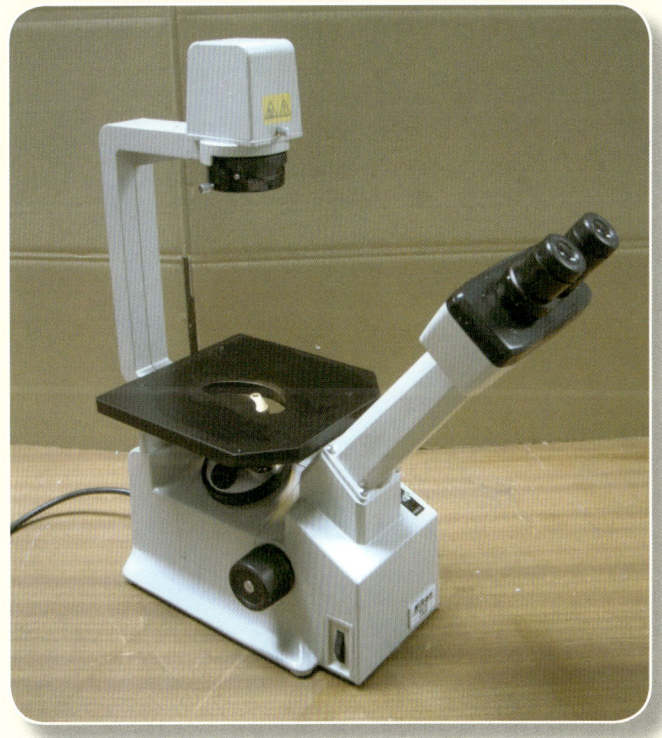

specimen and is sitting on the stage rather than looking at the specimen from the top. The inverted microscopes are often used for looking at living organisms, tissue cultures and cell cultures.

# LIGHT AND COLOUR

## Refracting telescope

The refracting telescope uses a lens to gather and focus light. The first telescopes built were refractors. The small telescopes sold in department stores are refractors, as well as, those used for rifle scopes. Refracting telescopes are rugged. After the initial alignment, their optical system is more resistant to misalignment than the reflector telescopes. The glass surface inside the tube is sealed from the atmosphere so it rarely needs cleaning. Since the tube is closed off from the outside, air currents and effects due to changing temperatures are eliminated. This means that the images are steadier and sharper than those from a reflecting telescope of the same size.

## Reflecting telescope

The reflecting telescope uses a mirror to gather and focus light. All celestial objects (including those in our solar system) are so far away that all of the light rays coming from them reach the Earth as parallel rays. Because the light rays are parallel to each other, the reflector telescope's mirror has a parabolic shape. The parabolic-shaped mirror focuses the parallel lights rays to a single point. All modern research telescopes and large amateur ones are of the reflector type because of its advantages over the refractor telescope. Reflecting telescopes do not suffer from chromatic aberration because all wavelengths will reflect off the mirror in the same way. These telescopes are cheaper to make than refractors of the same size. In a telescope, we get a highly magnified, real, inverted image with respect to the object.

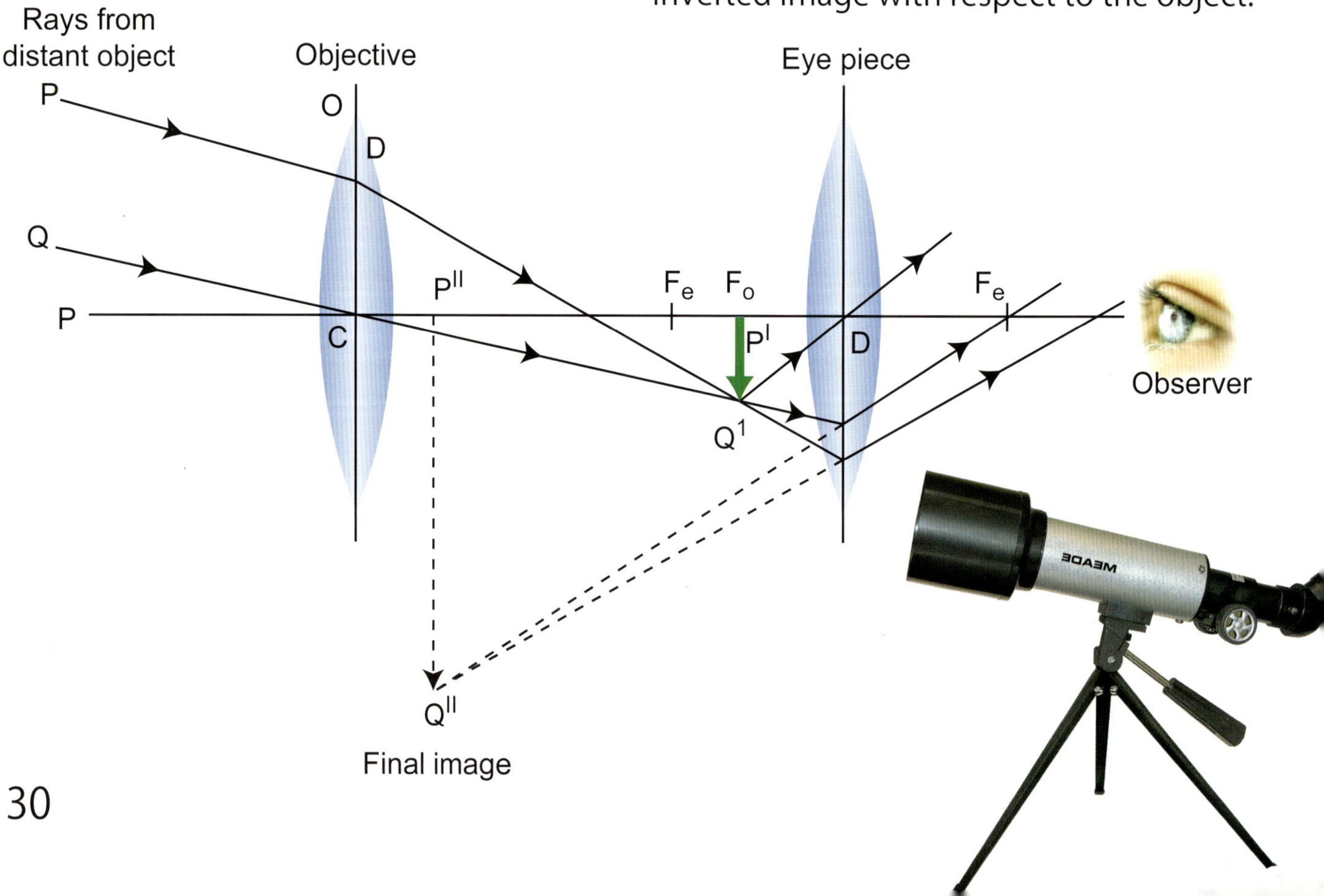

# Test Your Memory

1. Why is the sky blue?

2. Write three properties of light?

3. What do you understand by dispersion?

4. What is total internal reflection?

5. What are the constituent colours of white light?

6. What is the law of reflection?

7. Give one example of optical mirage?

8. What happens when light strikes at the surface of a plane mirror?

9. What is the difference between convex and concave lens?

10. Write the uses of various types of mirrors?

11. What is a microscope?

12. What are the different types of telescopes?

**LIGHT AND COLOUR**

# Index

## A
angle of incidence  6, 8, 9, 11, 15, 19, 20
angle of reflection  8, 19
angle of refraction  9
Anthony Van Leeuwenhoek  26

## B
binoculars  11

## C
centre of curvature  20, 21, 22
coarse and knobs  27
coaxial focus knobs  27
compound microscope  26, 27
concave lens  24
concave mirrors  17, 18, 20
converging lens  25
convex lens  24, 25
convex mirrors  17, 18, 22
critical angle  6, 10, 11, 15

## D
density  5, 6
diffraction  7
dispersion  6, 7, 12, 14, 15
diverging lenses  24

## E
electromagnetic wave  3
energy  3, 8
eyepiece lens  27

## F
focus  18, 20, 21, 22, 23, 24, 25, 26, 27, 30
frequency  3, 9

## G
Galileo Galilei  28

## H
halos  11
Hans Lippershey  28
hypermytropia  25

## I
illuminator  27
interference of light  7
iris Diaphragm  27

## J
Jacob Metius  28

## K
kaleidoscopes  18, 23

## L
Laws of refraction  9
lenses  6, 8, 9, 24, 25, 26, 27, 28
light  3, 4, 5, 6, 7, 8, 9, 10, 11, 12, 13, 14, 15, 16, 17, 18, 19, 21, 22, 23, 24, 25, 27, 28, 29, 30

## M
magnetic fields  3
magnifying lenses  6
microscopes  6, 26, 27, 29
microscopy  26
myopia  24

## N
nosepiece  27

## O
objective lens  27
optical illusion  16
optical phenomenon  10, 16

## P
periscopes  11, 18
plain mirror  17
pole  20, 21, 22
principal axis  20, 21, 22, 24, 25
prism  3, 6, 12, 13, 14
projectors  18

## R
rainbow  3, 6, 7, 10, 14, 15, 16, 23
reflecting surface  8
reflecting telescope  28, 30
reflection  5, 6, 7, 8, 10, 11, 14, 19, 20, 22
refracting telescope  28, 30
refraction  6, 7, 10, 13, 16, 24, 25
refraction index  10

## S
solar cookers  18

## T
telescope  28, 30
total internal reflection  6, 10, 11, 15

## V
VIBGYOR  13, 14
visible light  3, 14, 28
visible spectrum  3, 12

## W
wave energy  8
wavelength  3, 4, 9, 10, 12, 13
waves  3, 7, 9

## Z
Zaccharias Hanssen  26